Pra
A Challenge
to Overcome

Cardinal Angelo Comastri

Preface by Pope Francis

NOTES ON PRAYER
Volume 1

*All booklets are published
thanks to the generosity of the supporters
of the Catholic Truth Society*

CATHOLIC
TRUTH
SOCIETY

Notes on Prayer Series

Volume 1 *Prayer Today: A Challenge to Overcome*

Volume 2 *Praying with the Psalms*

Volume 3 *The Prayer of Jesus*

Volume 4 *Praying with Saints and Sinners*

Volume 5 *The Parables of Prayer*

Volume 6 *The Church in Prayer*

Volume 7 *The Prayer of Mary and the Saints Who Met Her*

Volume 8 *The Prayer Jesus Taught Us: Our Father*

All biblical quotations are taken from the ESV-CE Bible.

© *Dicastero per l'Evangelizzazione – Sezione per le questioni fondamentali dell'evangelizzazione nel mondo – Libreria Editrice Vaticana.*

English edition © 2024 The Incorporated Catholic Truth Society, 42-46 Harleyford Road, London SE11 5AY. Tel: 020 7640 0042. www.ctsbooks.org

ISBN 978 1 78469 825 6

Contents

Preface by Pope Francis

Prayer is the breath of faith, its most proper expression. It's like a silent cry that comes out from the heart of whoever trusts and believes in God. It's not easy to find words to express this mystery. How many definitions of prayer we can gather from the saints and masters of spirituality, as well as from the reflections of theologians! Nevertheless, it is always and only in the simplicity of those who live prayer that prayer finds expression. The Lord, moreover, warned us that, when we pray, we must not waste words, deluding ourselves that thus we will be heard. He taught us rather to prefer silence and to entrust ourselves to the Father, who knows the kind of things we need even before we ask for them (see *Matt* 6:7-8).

The Ordinary Jubilee of 2025 is already at the door. How to prepare ourselves for this event, so important for the life of the Church, if not by means of prayer? The year 2023 was set aside for a rediscovery of the conciliar teachings, contained especially in the four Constitutions of Vatican II. It is a way of keeping alive the mandate that the Fathers gathered at the Council wished to place in our hands, so that by means of its implementation, the Church might recover its youthful face and proclaim, in a language adapted to the men and women of our time, the beauty of the faith.

Now is the time to prepare for the year 2024, a year that will be dedicated entirely to prayer. In our own time the need is being felt more and more strongly for a true spirituality capable of responding to the great questions which confront us every day of our lives, questions caused by a global scenario that is far from serene. The ecological-economic-social crisis aggravated by the recent pandemic; wars, especially the one in Ukraine, which sow death, destruction, and poverty; the culture of indifference and waste that tends to stifle aspirations for peace and solidarity and keeps God at the margins of personal and social life… These phenomena combine to bring about a ponderous atmosphere that holds many people back from living with joy and serenity. What we need, therefore, is that our prayer should rise up with greater insistence to the Father so that He will listen to the voice of those who turn to Him, confident of being heard.

This year dedicated to prayer is in no way intended to affect the initiatives which every particular Church considers it must plan for its own daily pastoral commitment. On the contrary, it aims to recall the foundation on which the various pastoral plans should be developed and find consistency. This is a time when, as individuals or communities, we can rediscover the joy of praying in a variety of forms and expressions. A time of consequence enabling us to increase the certainty of our faith and trust in the intercession of the Virgin Mary and the saints. In short, a year in which we can have the experience almost of a "school of prayer", without taking anything for granted, (or at cut-rate,) especially with regard to our way of praying, but making our own every day the words of the disciples when they asked Jesus: "Lord, teach us to pray" (*Luke* 11:1).

In this year we are invited to become more humble and to leave space for the prayer that flows from the Holy Spirit. It is He who knows how to put into our hearts and onto our lips the right words so that we will be heard by the Father. Prayer in the Holy Spirit is what unites us with Jesus and allows us to adhere to the will of the Father. The Spirit is the interior Teacher who indicates the way to follow. Thanks to Him the prayer of even just one person can become the prayer of the entire Church, and vice versa. There is nothing like prayer according to the Spirit to make Christians feel united as the one family of God. It is God who knows how to recognise everyone's needs and how to make those needs become the invocation and intercession of all.

I am certain that bishops, priests, deacons, and catechists will find more effective ways this year of placing prayer at the basis of the announcement of hope which the 2025 Jubilee intends to make resonate in this troubled time. For this reason, the contribution of consecrated persons will be of great value, particularly communities of contemplative life. I hope that in all the Shrines of the world, privileged places for prayer, initiatives should be increased so that every pilgrim can find an oasis of serenity and return with a heart filled with consolation. May prayer, both personal and communal, be unceasing, without interruption, according to the will of the Lord Jesus (see *Luke* 18:1), so that the Kingdom of God may spread, and the Gospel reach every person seeking love and forgiveness.

As an aid for this Year of Prayer, some short texts have been produced which, with their simple language, will make possible entry into the various dimensions of prayer. I thank the authors for their contribution and willingly place into your hands these 'notes' so that everyone can rediscover the beauty of trusting in the Lord with humility and joy. And don't forget to pray also for me.

Vatican City
27 September 2023

Franciscus

Introduction...A Must-Read!

———

As a preface, or rather, as an introduction to these pages on the fascinating and quite timely theme of prayer, I thought I would present to you the account of a singular experience of the Russian writer Alexander Solzhenitsyn. In 1962 he published his first novel and gave it the title *One Day in the Life of Ivan Denisovich*.

It was the euphoric period of de-Stalinisation. Khrushchev himself, before an assembly of intellectuals, judged Solzhenitsyn's work as one of those which "help the people in their struggle for the new society, unite and strengthen their forces."

The Russian writer's narrative tells us of one of the 3,653 days that Ivan Denisovich Shukhov must spend in the concentration camp, while pointing out that for the poor convict it is "a beautiful, almost happy day."

It is easy to guess that this poor Ivan is the author himself, who summarises, in this "beautiful, almost happy day," all the horror that was aroused in him by that place, where "a man can be turned inside out like a glove"; where, "after a day of wind, of frost, of hunger, a ladleful of cabbage soup counts more than the freedom of all past life and all future life and where, in the evening, the prisoner can be happy to have managed to survive."

Forced labour, being counted and recounted like sheep, the awareness of being at the mercy of a tyrant and not of justice, lead to the spiritual annihilation of man, to the undoing of his moral sense, making him evil, cruel, ruthless and selfish, to the point that "the prisoner's worst enemy is the prisoner himself."

But in the gloomy night of oppression, in what seems like the dominion of wolves, a small flame shines and gives hope: it is the Faith of a prisoner who has guarded, defended and propagated it; that of the young Alyoshka, who "looks at the sun and rejoices" and "has a smile on his lips," in spite of everything.

He has managed to bring with him, into that hell, a copy of the New Testament: the Gospels and the Letters of the Apostles; has, so far, spared it from the constant searches, and is happy. Every evening, in the dim light of the lamp that remains lit in the cold barracks, reads and prays. Ivan listens to him, his bunk being right above his. That evening he hears him say:

"After all, Ivan Denisovich, your soul wants to pray to God. Why don't you let it have its way?"

Shukhov gave Alyoshka a sidelong glance. His eyes were glowing like two candles. He sighed. "Because,

Alyoshka, prayers are like our written complaints. They either don't make it through, or they come back rejected."

"…Prayer must be persistent! And if you have faith, and you tell that mountain to move, it will move."

Shukhov grinned and rolled himself another cigarette. He got a light from one of the Estonians.

"Stop your chatter, Alyoshka!… In the Caucasus you prayed with your whole Baptist club, but did you move even one mountain?"

The poor yokels. They prayed to God, and what was the nuisance? Yet what they got for themselves, all of them, was twenty-five years apiece. Because that was how it was: twenty-five years for everybody.

"But we didn't pray for that, Denisovich," Alyoshka insisted. He came closer to Shukhov and held the Gospel up to his face. "The Lord has commanded us that of all earthly and passing things, we are to pray only for our daily bread: 'Give us this day our daily bread.'"

"The ration, you mean?" Shukhov said.

Alyoshka kept trying to persuade him, with his eyes more than his words, and he pressed and stroked his hand.

"Ivan Denisovich! You mustn't pray to get a package in the mail or an extra portion of gruel. What people esteem is vile to God! We must pray for the spirit, that the Lord may remove the scum of wickedness from our hearts."…

Shukhov lay down again… Lost in his own thoughts, he didn't hear what Alyoshka was mumbling about. "All in all," he finally said, "no matter how much you pray, they won't reduce your sentence. You'll have to serve it from reveille to lights out."

"But that's not to be prayed for!" Alyoshka was horrified. "What do you want with freedom? In freedom what's left of your faith will be choked with thorns! Be glad you're in prison! Here you have time to think about your soul."…

Shukhov looked up at the ceiling in silence. He himself didn't know whether he wanted freedom or not…. And where his life would be better – in here or on the outside – there was no telling….

Alyoshka wasn't lying when he said he was glad to be in prison. You could tell by his voice and his eyes….

"Look, Alyoshka," Shukhov explained, "you're onto something: Christ ordered you to prison, and for the sake of Christ you are here. But why am *I* here?"…

The question was left unanswered, interrupted by yet another nighttime check with its tally. And yet the answer had already been given: "We must pray for the spirit, that the Lord may remove the scum of wickedness from our hearts."

Wickedness is the true evil of man. To free himself from this is his task, without a doubt, but this is impossible for him without God's help: this is the great reason why man needs prayer. And wherever we may be, we must make Alyoshka's prayer our own: "Lord, remove the scum of wickedness from our hearts!"

How beautiful, how consoling, how true and quite timely is the testimony of this prisoner of a far-flung concentration camp of immense Russia! His lesson is also valid for us at this time: and, in particular, in this year dedicated to prayer.

ANGELO CARD. COMASTRI

Three Authoritative Reminders on the Need for Prayer

With prayer we can lift the world

St Thérèse of Lisieux (1873-1897), who was a wonderful and fruitful missionary despite always staying inside a convent, expressed well the secret of the fruitfulness of prayer, which many today no longer understand. She, with great lucidity, wrote:

"Give me a lever and a fulcrum on which to lean it," said Archimedes, "and I will lift the world."

What he could not obtain because his request had only a material end, without reference to God, the Saints have obtained in all its fullness. They lean on God Almighty's power itself and their lever is the prayer that inflames with love's fire. With this lever they have raised the world – with this lever the Saints of the Church Militant still raise it, and will raise it to the end of time." (St Thérèse of Lisieux, Mgr Thomas N Taylor (tr.), *Saint Thérèse of Lisieux, the Little Flower of Jesus*, Burns, Oates & Washbourne, London 1912, pp. 176-177).

These are words to meditate upon while kneeling. And, above all, they are words to be taken seriously when starting to truly pray. Now: today!

Thérèse hands over to us a truth of incalculable value: the true "apostles" are the saints! And they are apostles, first of all, because they pray!

In just a few words, she demolishes old controversies and sheds light on the problem of the evangelisation of the world and of the fruitfulness of the Christian apostolate: what is needed are saints!

And in order to have saints what is needed are people of authentic prayer, and authentic prayer is that which inflames with a fire of love: only in this way is it possible to lift the world and bring it near to the heart of God.

Could this have been put in a way more clear? And, at the same time, more simple? And more profound? And more radiantly evangelical?

St Thérèse of Lisieux, patron of the missions (note this!) understood the efficacy of prayer from the age of fourteen. Here is how matters went.

In France, on the night of 17 March 1887, a certain Henri Pranzini committed a triple murder. He was arrested, and his trial ended on 23 July with a death sentence, in keeping with French law at the time.

Thérèse of Lisieux, now a saint, was 14 years old at the time and was already a wonderful Christian, open to the light of God and eager to lead souls to encounter God's mercy.

As soon as she heard the news of Henri Pranzini's death sentence, Thérèse became very worried, because the murderer had expressly refused any meeting with a priest for absolution and everything suggested that he would die unrepentant.

The future saint was upset over this and began to pray fervently, getting her sister Céline to do likewise. And what happened? Let's listen to Thérèse's vivid account.

Need I say that in the depths of my heart I felt certain my request would be granted? But, that I might gain courage to persevere in the quest for souls, I said in all simplicity: "My God, I am quite sure that Thou wilt pardon this unhappy Pranzini. I should still think so if he did not confess his sins or give any sign of sorrow, because I have such confidence in Thy unbounded mercy; but this is my first sinner, and therefore I beg for just one sign of repentance to reassure me." My prayer was granted to the letter. My Father never allowed us to read the papers, but I did not think there was any disobedience in looking at the part about Pranzini. The day after his execution I hastily opened the paper, *La Croix*, and what did I see? Tears betrayed my emotion; I was obliged to run out of the room. Pranzini had mounted the scaffold without confessing or receiving absolution, and the executioners were already dragging him towards the fatal block, when all at once, apparently in answer to a sudden inspiration, he turned round, seized the crucifix which the Priest was offering to him, and kissed Our Lord's Sacred Wounds three times…. Then his soul went to receive the merciful sentence of Him who declares that in "heaven there is more joy for one sinner who repents than for ninety-nine righteous people who have no need of repentance" (*Lk* 15:7) (*ibid.*, pp. 73-74).

If we believed in the effectiveness of prayer, we would spend a lot of time on our knees. And the world would change direction!

Man cannot be fulfilled without prayer

David Maria Turoldo (1916-1992) said:

I believe that man cannot be fulfilled without silence and prayer. What is most lacking in our time, in this civilisation, is the spirit of prayer. This would be the true revolution: does the world not pray? I pray. Does the world not keep silent? I keep silent. And I set myself to listen.

Revolution does not consist in breaking or destroying, but in bringing a new spirit into the age-old forms.

What we lack most is precisely the relationship with the mystery, the opening into the infinity of God: this is why man is so alone, insufficient and threatened. It is the characteristic of this civilisation of noise: no more keeping silence, no more contemplation. The true value of things has been lost.

And it is a time without songs. Today there is no singing; today there is screaming and shouting: indeed, a civilisation of noise. A time without prayer. Without silence, and therefore without listening. Nobody listens to anyone anymore. It is not without reason that these times are joyless, because joy comes from very far off. There is a need to dig deep: it is necessary to return to prayer.

Yes, it is necessary to return to prayer! Only prayer gives God room in our lives and in the history of the world: and with God all things are possible.

Without God we are too poor to be able to help the poor

In 1968 I met Mother Teresa of Calcutta for the first time. I had been a priest for just a year and I felt the impulse to go to the Mother and ask her to accompany me with her prayer.

As soon as the Mother saw me, she asked me point blank, "How many hours a day do you pray?" I was a little taken aback, because I was expecting her to ask me, "How much charity do you do?" However, I replied, "Mother, I celebrate Holy Mass every day, I pray the Rosary every day, I never leave out the daily prayer of the Breviary…"

Mother Teresa took my hands in hers and then whispered in my ear, "It's not enough! The relationship with Jesus is a relationship of love! And in love one cannot limit oneself to duty. You do well to celebrate Mass every day, to pray the Rosary and the Breviary: it is your duty! But you must make a bit of room for adoration before the Eucharist: just you and Jesus!

Mother Teresa's advice went to my heart, but I ventured to say, "Mother, I expected you to ask me, How much charity do you do?" The Mother became serious and then slowly spoke these words which enclose the whole secret of her life. She said, "And do you believe that I could bring my love to the poor if Jesus did not give me His love every day through prayer? Remember: without God we are too poor to be able to help the poor!"

These profound words should be shouted in the churches and in the squares: they are the medicine to cure the disorientation of many people at present… including churchmen!

With her life, Mother Teresa reminds us of an indispensable truth: "Without God we are too poor to be able to help the poor!"

Let us draw out what follows from this: with honesty, with readiness, with consistency.

Prayer is a magnet that draws us to Jesus

Domenico Giuliotti, a poet and writer, was born on 18 February 1877 in San Casciano Val di Pesa, in the province of Florence. He had a peaceful childhood, in a family in which the Catholic faith was in the air they breathed. He himself says:

My childhood, spent in an old secluded villa on the top of a hill, was very religious. The countryside was still pious, and I was surrounded with truly pure things and people. It was a time when the farmers, after the day's toil, gathered in the kitchen, lit up by a blaze in the hearth, and, kneeling on the uneven floor, said the Rosary, while in a large pan the fragrant seasonings for their black bread soup were simmering. My father, an overseer, was friend and father to those under him. My mother, born into a peasant family, a very pure and solid woman, alternated the management of the household with daily prayer. In the morning a brief thanksgiving to the Lord for having granted us a good rest and the invocation of His help for the work of the day; at midday the *Angelus Domini* before sitting down to table; and, before going to bed, the Hail Mary and the Creed. They were prayers that we all said together and that struck down into our souls like a wholesome light. (*La Civiltà Cattolica*, 1975 III, pp. 495 ff.).

Later, in his adolescence, Domenico Giuliotti wrenched himself away from Christ and became a ferocious enemy of the Church and of everything that smacked of Christianity: he became – as he himself would say – a follower of the Antichrist.

But his heart was restless and, little by little, he set off on the road of return. Once he had taken the step that brought him back to the household of the faith,

Domenico Giuliotti realised what a "madman" he had been and became inflexible with himself in punishment for his inexcusable desertion.

He behaved like the drunk who, once he has cut his ties with wine, no longer wants even to smell it. Domenico Giuliotti, after his conversion, viscerally loved the Catholic faith and wrote vibrant pages in defence of the greatness of the Catholic priest. Here is one memorable page:

> They alone [the priests], even if unworthy, give support, with Christ supporting them, to the tottering walls of the earthly city. If we imagine that they have disappeared, there is no more Church; but if there is no more Church, there is no more liturgy; and if there is no more liturgy, there are no more sacraments; and if there are no more sacraments, there is no more irrigation of grace.
>
> And so drought, sterility, death. The priest is a man, but he is more than the angels; he is a sinner, but he forgives sins; he is a servant, but the Lord obeys him. The angels, and even the Queen of the angels, do not have the power to absolve, nor to compel Christ every day to renew, under the sacred species of bread and wine, the universally reparative offering of God to God. He, he alone can work these wonders. (*Polvere dell'esilio*, Vallecchi, Florence 1929, p. 129).

Domenico Giuliotti died a Christian death at 9:15 am on 12 January 1956. Shortly before dying he had written:

So come quickly, O Lord, to devour all evil, with your ravenous love. What does it matter if my weary eyes of flesh will not see you? I know you will come, Lord! I can, therefore, happily depart from this 'bloody little plot,' now that, in proportion to my ability to understand, that is, to love, you have disclosed and unveiled to me your adorable Mystery. (*Il malpensante: pagine di fede e di lotta e d'amore*, Vallecchi, Florence 1957, p. 166).

How did it come about, the miracle of Domenico Giuliotti's return to his heartfelt embrace with God? One day he himself gave the answer: "It all happened through the earnest and insistent prayers of my mother."

It's true! When someone converts, there is always somewhere one who is praying!

Lord, Teach Us to Pray!

Without prayer one cannot live

The Bible clearly affirms the need for prayer: for true prayer!

In the Old Testament, first of all, there are two episodes that shed abundant light on the enormous power of prayer.

The first is set by the oaks of Mamre. Abraham has just hosted three mysterious figures and has received the unprecedented announcement that, within a year, he will be the father of a child…long awaited. The setting is full of mystery, but also dense with light: every encounter with God, in fact, is like this.

Here is the scene of the bold and insistent prayer:

> Then the men set out from there, and they looked down towards Sodom. And Abraham went with them to set them on their way. The Lord said, "Shall I hide from Abraham what I am about to do, seeing that Abraham shall surely become a great and mighty nation, and all the nations of the earth shall be blessed in him?" (*Gen* 18:16-18).

God confides to Abraham that sin weighs on the fate of two cities, to the point that He is about to destroy them. Abraham feels a stirring of solidarity on behalf of the two cities and, at the same time, feels that he can sway the hearts of the "three mysterious figures":

> Then Abraham drew near and said, "Will you indeed sweep away the righteous with the wicked? Suppose there are fifty righteous within the city. Will you then sweep away the place and not spare it for the fifty righteous who are in it? Far be it from you to do such a thing, to put the righteous to death with the wicked, so that the righteous fare as the wicked! Far be that from you! Shall not the Judge of all the earth do what is just?" (*Gen* 18:23-25).

True prayer ushers one into the Heart of God, such that one can afford to be bold and insistent. This is why Abraham does not lose hope and goes down to forty people, to thirty, to twenty and the answer is, "For the sake of twenty I will not destroy it" (*Gen* 18:31). Abraham has a moment of hesitation, but then, with the courage of faith, he dares to say, "'Oh let not the Lord be angry, and I will speak again but this once. Suppose ten are found there.' He answered, 'For the sake of ten I will not destroy it'" (*Gen* 18:32).

The ten righteous, unfortunately, were not to be found! But the meaning of the story remains intact: prayer is dialogue; prayer is an initiative of love; prayer is boldness; prayer is the door that ushers us into the Heart of God and into the very mystery of His decisions.

Oh, if we would truly pray! John Paul I, in one of the few catecheses that the Lord granted him, exclaimed with his usual candour, "We lose many battles because we pray so little!" The Bible thoroughly agrees.

The second memorable episode on the power of prayer is in the book of Exodus. Israel is journeying to the Promised Land, but the journey is full of snares, dangers, ambushes, enemies. Faced with one powerful and insidious enemy, Moses makes the following decision:

> So Moses said to Joshua, "Choose for us men, and go out and fight with Amalek. Tomorrow I will stand on the top of the hill with the staff of God in my hand." So Joshua did as Moses told him, and fought with Amalek, while Moses, Aaron, and Hur went up to the top of the hill. Whenever Moses held up his hand, Israel prevailed, and whenever he lowered his hand, Amalek prevailed. But Moses's hands grew weary, so they took a stone and put it under him, and he sat on it, while Aaron and Hur held up his hands, one on one side, and the other on the other side. So his hands were steady until the going down of the sun. (*Ex* 17:9-12).

Sometimes, faced with the continuous problems of our toilsome journey on the way towards Paradise, we seek solutions of pure human alchemy and, at times, of entirely earthly cunning.

What if the solution, instead, were simply to raise one's hands towards Heaven day and night? Could it be possible that the example of Moses has something to teach us too, "professors" of God rather than "witnesses" of God?

In theory we are all convinced of the importance of prayer: there is much talk of this, and it is repeated everywhere.

But are we really sure that prayer is at the centre of our lives? It is one thing to talk about prayer, another thing to pray!

Sometimes, faced with the recurring and insidious challenges of history, we are all tempted to trust in the initiatives of the consummately skilled and highly professional...in theory. And what if, instead, we simply looked for a few people, like Aaron and Hur, to keep always raised the hands of those who must pray for all, do we not think that we would have more strength and more credibility and more incisiveness in our apostolate?

"Jesus prayed!": the end-all argument for prayer

The conduct of Jesus is, for the disciple, an absolute norm of life. Jesus, in fact, is the Master!

Well then, no one can deny that prayer was truly the centre of Jesus's life: prayer was His breath, His horizon of reference, the wellspring of His deeds and words.

Blaise Pascal (1623-1662), looking to Jesus, drew from Him the norms of Christian conduct and concluded,

"I love poverty, because Christ loved poverty!" But the same can easily and legitimately be said about prayer: I love prayer, no need to think twice, because Christ loved prayer!

The evangelist Mark notes, "And rising very early in the morning, while it was still dark, he departed and went out to a desolate place, and there he prayed." (*Mark* 1:35).

It must have been such a habitual gesture as to have been deeply imprinted in the memory of the apostles: after the Ascension, they could not remember their Lord and Master without also remembering His prayer.

St Luke, a writer able almost to bring before the reader's eyes the actions of Jesus's life, underlines a detail of great importance: Jesus, before making the decision to call the apostles, spent a whole night in prayer! The evangelist relates this fact because it is an extraordinary life lesson: "In these days he went out to the mountain to pray, and all night he continued in prayer to God. And when day came, he called his disciples and chose from them twelve" (*Luke* 6:12-13).

Charles de Foucauld (1858-1916), deeply touched by this conduct of Jesus, fell in love with nocturnal prayer: for him the night became the customary refuge of his prayer and his most beloved time for conversation, adoration and intercession.

Shouldn't every disciple do the same? Shouldn't a disciple always have his eyes turned towards the Master to discern every heartbeat, every nuance, every attitude in His life? How much, today, is our gaze turned to the Lord? How much does His life inspire our lives? These questions cannot be avoided if we want Jesus to be the Master and ourselves the disciples!

It is, however, painful to have to admit that many of our decisions do not come from prayer: they come from the intellect, but is the intellect enough? They come from study, but is study enough? They come from research, but is research enough? They come from sociology, but is sociology enough? They come from shrewdness, but is shrewdness enough?

Let us again follow the Master. The evangelist Matthew writes, "Now when Jesus heard this [of the death of John the Baptist], he withdrew from there in a boat to a desolate place by himself" (*Matt* 14:13); a little further on, he adds:

> Immediately [after the multiplication of the loaves] he made the disciples get into the boat and go before him to the other side, while he dismissed the crowds. And after he had dismissed the crowds, he went up on the mountain by himself to pray. When evening came, he was there alone. (*Matt* 14:22-23).

These habitual actions of Jesus remained indelibly engraved in the memory of the disciples and became a constant point of reference for their decisions and conduct.

How could Peter (the one Jesus chose to confirm the faith of the others!) have said one day, "We will devote ourselves to prayer and to the ministry of the word" (*Acts* 6:4), had he not been more than convinced that he was following the example he had seen the Master set?

Doesn't Peter's decision have something to say to us today?

I am convinced that today the beginning of the sixth chapter of the Acts of the Apostles should be meditated upon at length: I have the impression that we are moving in the direction opposite to that which the apostles took at a time very similar to ours.

The Gospels even tell us that Jesus's prayer led to a crisis of prayer for the disciples. Watching Jesus pray, they realised that they did not know how to pray! And this is what happened: "Now Jesus was praying in a certain place, and when he finished, one of his disciples said to him, 'Lord, teach us to pray'" (*Luke* 11:1).

Teach us to pray!

Jesus's prayer must have been at once transparent and mysterious: it was prayer in which something beautiful was seen, but at the same time it concealed a profound mystery. The apostles' request was spontaneous: "Jesus, bring us into this beautiful mystery, which shines through in your eyes and on your face. Jesus, teach us to pray!"

We too need to take up this invocation: in fact, we must all get it clear in our heads that the journey of our prayer is not over, because the journey of faith is not over and the journey of conversion is not over;

the journey of conversion, the journey of faith and the journey of prayer are simultaneous journeys, they are interchangeable journeys.

The evangelist John, who had the grace of hearing the beating of Christ's heart and of sensing the abyss of Love that it concealed, photographed the sentiments of the last hours of Christ's life by relating a long and memorable prayer: the prayer to the Father, the prayer of the offering of Love, the prayer of divine friendship, the heartfelt prayer for the unity of the disciples, the prayer to invoke the soul of prayer for the apostles and for the disciples of all times.

Once the supper was ended, St Luke relates:

> And he came out and went, as was his custom, to the Mount of Olives, and the disciples followed him. And when he came to the place, he said to them, "Pray that you may not enter into temptation." And he withdrew from them about a stone's throw, and knelt down and prayed. (*Luke* 22:39-41).

Could it be possible that Jesus, at the most dramatic moment of His life, when His own body reacted by sweating blood, saw His only strength and resource in prayer? Yet it is so! The Gospel cannot be changed, nor can it be retouched: it is so, simply so!

When the supreme moment had come, Jesus, praying, entered into the embrace of the Father: "Then Jesus, calling out with a loud voice, said, 'Father, into your hands I commit my spirit!' And having said this he breathed his last" (*Luke* 23:46).

If such was the life of Jesus, if such was His apostolate, can we live a different life from Him or think differently about our apostolate?

"Lord, teach us to pray!"

The Word of God answers us. Let us listen!

⸺◈⸺

Man's first step towards prayer

O LORD, you have shown me my end,
how short is the length of my days.
Now I know how fleeting is my life. (*Ps* 39:4)

The Bible categorically teaches (but experience also teaches!) that man is small. Yes, man is small!

This truth at the outset is fundamental. In fact, if man exchanges the real measure of his stature with the unreal measure of his desires, he makes a fatal mistake and, sooner or later, he will pass from illusion to disappointment: he will pass from the delirium of omnipotence to the prostration of nihilism. This is what has happened and continues to happen: look around!

The Bible faithfully informs us: man is small! The first attitude, then, that allows us to begin a true journey of prayer is precisely this: the recognition of our smallness, the awareness of our condition as creatures.

Let's look at a few significant texts of Scripture, through which the true face of man clearly emerges.

Isaiah, with clear and robust language, writes, "A voice says, 'Cry!' And I said, 'What shall I cry?' All flesh is grass, and all its beauty is like the flower of the field. (*Isa* 40:6).

It's true! Man carries within himself an innate incompleteness, which is nothing other than his very condition as a "creature" written in all the fibres of his being: this is why man has an innate need for worship! Man's fatal danger is to mistake the object of worship!

Psalm 8, after recognising that man has within himself a mark of greatness, is quick to clarify:

> When I see the heavens, the work of your fingers,
> the moon and the stars which you arranged,
> what is man that you should keep him in mind.
> (vv. 4-5).

Psalm 37, taking up an objection both ancient and recent, advises:

> Do not fret because of the wicked;
> do not envy those who do evil,
> for they wither quickly like grass
> and fade like the green of the fields. (vv. 1-2).

Why? Because the wicked is the one who does not rely on the Lord; the wicked is the one who has directed his innate need for worship to "other lords": he will, inexorably, find himself crumpled up in emptiness and existential failure. For this reason, addressing the righteous, the psalmist whispers:

> Trust in the LORD and do good;
> then you will dwell in the land and find safe pasture.
> Find your delight in the LORD,
> who grants your heart's desire. (*ibid.*, vv. 3-4).

The psalmist is entirely assured in stating that only God is proportionate to the desires of the human heart: man, in fact, is thirsty for God! This is why the conclusion strikes home like an arrow:

> Better the few possessions of the upright,
> than the abundant wealth of the wicked;
> for the arms of the wicked shall be broken,
> and the LORD will support the upright.
> (*ibid.*, vv. 16-17).

Yet often it seems the righteous is a loser and the wicked is a winner. No, the psalmist assures! Don't be fooled:

> have seen the wicked one triumphant,
> towering like a cedar of Lebanon.
> I passed by again; he was gone.
> I searched; he was nowhere to be found.
> (*ibid.*, vv. 35-36).

This is the certainty of the man of faith, of the man who knows he is small and incomplete, but, at the same time, knows that God is his completeness!

Psalm 73, in a few lines, also conveys the same message:

As for me, my feet came close to stumbling;
my steps had almost slipped,
for I was filled with envy of the proud,
when I saw how the wicked prosper....

How suddenly they come to their ruin,
swept away, destroyed by terrors.
Like a dream one wakes from, O Lord,
when you wake you dismiss them as phantoms....

What else have I in heaven but you?
Apart from you, I want nothing on earth.
My flesh and my heart waste away;
God is the strength of my heart,
my portion for ever. (vv. 2-3, 19-20, 25-26).

This is the true face of man, which emerges from Scripture!

Man is a runt who cannot play at being a giant. For man, in fact, there is just one way out of his smallness: to lean on the only Great One and welcome His embrace. This is why Fyodor Dostoevsky, in a few dazzling words, said, "The one essential condition of human existence is that man should always be able to bow down before something infinitely great" (Fyodor Dostoevsky, Constance Garnett (tr.), *The Possessed*, Macmillan, New York 1913, p. 624). Gandhi wisely added, "The seeker after truth should be humbler than the dust" (MK Gandhi, *An Autobiography*, Navajivan Publishing House, Ahmedabad 1926, p. 7).

And St Agostino Roscelli, a great little Genoese priest of the nineteenth century, stated with profound theological precision, "In Paradise we will find people who were not martyrs, nor were they bishops, nor were they priests, nor were they theologians…but we will not find a single person who was not humble."

Without humility, one cannot come to God: only if man serenely accepts his smallness as a point of truth and point of departure for the journey of his restless intellect will he come to hear the steps of the Eternal and feel the caress of the Infinite.

Unfortunately, this doesn't always happen. Historical man, in fact, has experienced the tragic incident of freedom become pride: historical man has rejected God and, dramatically, has slipped into the bitter experience of sin. Here, then, is the indispensable second step.

―――

Man's second step towards prayer

God, be merciful to me, a sinner!
(*Luke* 18:13)

Friedrich Nietzsche (1844-1900), a disturbing philosopher and singular witness of the drama of Western culture, in *The Joyful Wisdom*, at fragment 108, confidently declares, "God is dead: but as the human race is constituted, there will perhaps be caves for millenniums yet, in which people will show his shadow. And we – we have still to overcome his shadow!" (Friedrich Nietzsche, Thomas Common (tr.), *The Complete Works of Friedrich Nietzsche*, vol. X, TN Foulis, Edinburgh 1910, p. 151).

A mad suggestion! God, in fact, will never become a shadow, while man becomes a shadow when he separates himself from God! Nietzsche himself, in fragment 125 of the same work, leaves to us a painful page in which atheism is no longer presented as an achievement, but as the highest drama. He writes:

Have you ever heard of the madman who on a bright morning lighted a lantern and ran to the market-place calling out unceasingly: "I seek God! I seek God!" As there were many people standing about who did not believe in God, he caused a great deal of amusement. Why! Is he lost? said one. Has he strayed away like a child? said another. Or does he keep himself hidden? Is he afraid of us? Has he taken a sea-voyage? Has he emigrated? the people cried out laughingly, all in a hubbub. The insane man jumped into their midst and transfixed them with his glances. "Where is God gone?" he called out. "I mean to tell you! We have killed him – you and I! We are all his murderers! But how have we done it? How were we able to drink up the sea? Who gave us the sponge to wipe away the whole horizon? What did we do when we loosened this earth from its sun? Whither does it now move?

Whither do we move? Away from all suns? Do we not dash on unceasingly? Backwards, sideways, forwards, in all directions? Is there still an above and below? Do we not stray, as through infinite nothingness? Does not empty space breathe upon us? Has it not become colder? Does not night come on continually, darker and darker? Shall we not have to light lanterns in the morning? Do we not hear the noise of the grave-diggers who are burying God? Do we not smell the divine putrefaction? – for even Gods putrefy! God is dead! God remains dead! And we have killed him! How shall we console ourselves, the most murderous of all murderers? The holiest and the mightiest that the world has hitherto possessed, has bled to death under our knife – who will wipe the blood from us? With what water could we cleanse ourselves? What lustrums, what sacred games shall we have to devise? Is not the magnitude of this deed too great for us?" (ibid., pp. 167-168).

Paradoxically, Nietzsche did grasp a real and tragic aspect of human history: man, in fact, has tried and is truly trying to kill God; man has tried and is trying to flee from his Father; man has tried and is trying to make a 'god' of his own: indeed, he is trying to make himself 'god'!

And the result? The result is the bitter arrival at a sense of orphanhood, at an oppressive insignificance, at a loss of the co-ordinates that allow him to answer the decisive and unavoidable questions: Who are we? Where do we come from? Where are we going?

The journalist Indro Montanelli (1909-2001) was perfectly right when, shortly before his death, he had the courage and honesty to say:

> "If I must close my eyes without knowing where I come from and where I am going, and what I came to do in these hasty days of my life…was it worth it for me to open my eyes? What I am saying is a declaration of failure!"

This is something to think about.

Sin is an authentic seed of madness, which renders man's past and future mute and his present indecipherable: having rejected God, in fact, man finds himself in a pit of desires, which no longer lead to anything. This is the experience of many people today!

Psalm 78, grasping the wayward movement of all sin, goes so far as to compare it to a shot that misses the target: the Israelites "turned away and acted treacherously like their fathers; they twisted like a deceitful bow." (v. 57).

So sin is the true evil of man: it is the underlying evil from which all other evil stems. Jeremiah, in a very dense page, goes so far as to write, "What wrong did your fathers find in me that they went far from me, and went after worthlessness, and became worthless?" (2:5).

And, with a heartfelt appeal, he adds, "Your wickedness will chasten you, and your apostasy will reprove you.

Know and see that it is evil and bitter for you to forsake the Lord your God" (2:19).

Pier Paolo Pasolini (1922–1975), whom we can consider as a man emblematic of the modernity that has distanced itself from God, came to this bitter consideration:

> Something is always missing, there is a void
> in all my understanding. And it is vulgar,
> this not being complete, it is vulgar.
> Never was I so vulgar as in this anxiety,
> in this "not having Christ."
> ("L'alba meridionale" in *Le poesie*, Milan,
> Garzanti, 1975, p. 505).

All this is written: let us open our eyes and not repeat the same fatal mistakes.

But now comes a decisive question: how much does all this affect our journey of prayer? Evidently, a true journey of prayer cannot begin if there is not a clear and painful awareness of how much sin has wounded the heart of man and has devastated his history. We must in fact be well aware that at birth we find ourselves introduced into a humanity marked by the weight of the first sin, which opened the first wound of separation from God: and to this first sin (the original sin) has been added poison upon poison, to the point that human history has become ever more crooked, ever more twisted, ever more sick.

But it doesn't end here. On top of this inheritance of our birth is heaped the weight of our personal sin: alas, how we have left the weeds to flourish in the little field of our life!

Here then is the second step in the journey of prayer: becoming aware that our innate smallness has become entangled in sin, which has marred our original beauty and complicated our innate gravitation towards God, making our life an utter tangle.

Without this awareness, prayer cannot be true: to pray in truth, we must present ourselves before God with the open wounds of our smallness and our sin. Only in this way will the encounter with God be an encounter of liberation and redemption.

But here another question arises: does God want to set us free? Does God want to save us? Is God really interested in our pursuits and our misfortunes?

In the Old Testament there is a prayer that expresses the noblest and deepest aspiration of the human heart: "Oh that you would rend the heavens and come down, that the mountains might quake at your presence" (*Isa* 64:1).

And God? And His answer? Is there an answer from God? We Christians say, Yes!

God's first step towards man

For God so loved the world that he gave his only Son
(John 3:16)

It is only with this that Christian prayer begins: in fact we Christians, amid the onslaught of the ages, are a poor and rumpled flag, but we have news that, for two thousand years, has burned in our hearts and given light to our eyes: "And the Word became flesh and dwelt among us" (*John* 1:14).

Everything changes! All is lit up! Even sin (which the Church has the sacrosanct duty to preach and recall, because it is the 'serious thing' of human history), even sin no longer strikes fear: suddenly it is lit up by a ray of hope!

In one beautiful page, Blaise Pascal condenses all Christian teaching. Turning to God, he prays to Him with trust: "O God, reveal to me my sins."

But God hesitates, and does not wish to speak. Yet, faced with Pascal's insistence, He replies, "If you knew your sins, you would lose heart!"

Pascal, at this point, is troubled. He feels laid bare by the light of God, but has the strength to reply, "My God, then am I condemned to lose heart?"

And here is God's answer, which in the end is the synthesis of the whole Christian message: "No, you will not lose heart, because your sins will be revealed to you in the very moment they are forgiven!"

How true all this is! Jesus, coming into the world, dealt decisive blows to the stubborn pride of men.

Pride, in fact, blinds! Pride kills! Pride hides the wound and leaves it to fester.

We must approach Jesus with the truth of what we are: we are small and we are sinners! But here is the wonder: in the face of humility, God manifests an irrepressible desire for forgiveness and reconciliation. The evangelist John writes:

> For God did not send his Son into the world to condemn the world, but in order that the world might be saved through him. Whoever believes in him is not condemned, but whoever does not believe is condemned already, because he has not believed in the name of the only Son of God. And this is the judgement: the light has come into the world, and people loved the darkness rather than the light because their works were evil. For everyone who does wicked things hates the light and does not come to the light, lest his works should be exposed. But whoever does what is true comes to the light, so that it may be clearly seen that his works have been carried out in God. (*John* 3:17-21).

What, then, is Christian prayer?

Christian prayer is the ever new amazement of those who have found out that God has truly rent the heavens and become close to each of us. Christian prayer is the heartfelt weeping of the son who, oppressed by guilt, returns to the Father's house; and before the Father he lifts his gaze and does not find anger, but sees the smile and feels the infinite tenderness of the Father's Heart. Christian prayer begins like this.

The experience of joyful amazement is the soul of all authentic Christian prayer, so I understand why St Francis of Assisi, before the Crucifix, could not hold back his tears; I understand why Charles de Foucauld, in the Sahara desert, spent endless nights in front of the Eucharist just to feel Love and bless Love!

Jesus, in fact, is the good news of God's Love; indeed, Jesus is Love becomes good news!

But here we come to God's second step towards us; here we come to the summit of Christian prayer: God not only forgives us, but, in embracing us, gives us the gift of being able to love as He loves!

※※※

God's second step towards man

I made known to them your name, and I will continue to make it known, that the love with which you have loved me may be in them, and I in them.
(*John* 17:26)

We are at the very heart of the Christian experience: we are at the heart of prayer! To love as God loves? Yes, Christianity lies entirely here!

Let us follow the Master and listen to His Word: He alone can tell us how God loves.

One day Jesus, embittered by the continuous incomprehension and heedless hostility with which the news of God's goodness was repaid, said:

> "What man of you, having a hundred sheep, if he has lost one of them, does not leave the ninety-nine in the open country, and go after the one that is lost, until he finds it? And when he has found it, he lays it on his shoulders, rejoicing. And when he comes home, he calls together his friends and his neighbours, saying to them, 'Rejoice with me, for I have found my sheep that was lost.'" (*Luke* 15:4-6).

How human is this shepherd, who faces hardships, dangers, weariness to look for a lost sheep!

Instead, we must conclude: how divine this shepherd is! In fact, Jesus is quick to clarify: "Just so, I tell you, there will be more joy in heaven over one sinner who repents than over ninety-nine righteous persons who need no repentance" (*Luke* 15:7).

Behind the image of the shepherd, there is the face and the heart of God! It is a stunning fact!

Jesus adds a second brushstroke:

> "Or what woman, having ten silver coins, if she loses one coin, does not light a lamp and sweep the house and seek diligently until she finds it? And when she has found it, she calls together her friends

and neighbours, saying, 'Rejoice with me, for I have found the coin that I had lost.' Just so, I tell you, there is joy before the angels of God over one sinner who repents." (*Luke* 15:8-10).

This image of God is truly daring: God is like a woman who hits a rough patch when she realises she has lost a precious coin! The woman becomes agitated, runs around the house, sweeps and rummages everywhere until she shouts with joy at having found the lost coin.

Well, that's what God does! Jesus Himself says that there is joy before the angels of God over just one sinner who converts. God, then, has His joys, and Jesus points them out with no possibility of misunderstanding!

Don't they make us weep with emotion, these ways, this face and this heart of God?

But Jesus has not yet said it all: He makes a third vigorous brushstroke and the painting of the Father's Face takes on its definitive and most beautiful features:

"There was a man who had two sons; and the younger of them said to his father, 'Father, give me the share of property that is coming to me.' And he divided his property between them" (*Luke* 15:11-12).

Let us follow the quite delicate movement of the parable. At the centre is a father with a tragic fate: he has two sons; the younger has grown so insolent as to demand his inheritance while his father is still alive. This behaviour of the youngest son reveals a frightening cruelty: for this son the father is as if dead; indeed, this son kills the father within himself. He is only interested in the inheritance! And the father (imagine how wounded inside!) has to let his son run away. This father, in fact, truly loves and may not require his son to love him, since love cannot be commanded! The son leaves, but the castle in the air becomes a swinish life: it's always that way! Evil is evil because it does harm!

Jesus says:

> "Not many days later, the younger son gathered all he had and took a journey into a far country, and there he squandered his property in reckless living. And when he had spent everything, a severe famine arose in that country, and he began to be in need. So he went and hired himself out to one of the citizens of that country, who sent him into his fields to feed pigs." (*Luke* 15:13-15).

The dream is over: away from home things are bad; away from his father life is bitter; the alternative to home is the pigsty. Escape gives way to longing: longing for what? Longing for the father? Longing for an embrace? Longing to patch things up?

No, the parable does not recount these sentiments: it presents a rather drab picture of the younger son: "How many of my father's hired servants," he says, "have more than enough bread, but I perish here with hunger! I will arise and go to my father" (*Luke* 15:17-18).

In this son there is no remorse for having made his father suffer; there is no stinging wound that opens at the thought of how much pain he has caused his father's good heart. He does not say, weeping, "How I have made my father suffer! How I want to give him back the joy that I unjustly stole from him! How I love my father!"

No, the son has just the beginning of repentance and sets off slowly towards the house from which he had gone running.

But here is the unexpected thing! Here is the unexpected news, the news that jostles the son's heart: "But while he was still a long way off, his father saw him and felt compassion, and ran and embraced him and kissed him" (*Luke* 15:20).

How unpredictable this father is! How he stands apart from all human norms and judgements! He had the right to be indignant, he should have been sullen, and instead:

> "Bring quickly the best robe, and put it on him, and put a ring on his hand, and shoes on his feet. And bring the fattened calf and kill it, and let us eat and celebrate. For this my son was dead, and is alive again; he was lost, and is found." (*Luke* 15:22-24).

The father has not been changed by the test: he remains, unshakably, father! This father has a heart with an inexhaustible store of love: he knows only how to love and he loves totally and without conditions, because true love is necessarily maximalist and unconditional.

This father is God! It is staggering news. But it is news that does not come from us, but rather from the "only God, who is at the Father's side" (*John* 1:18).

Who can doubt? Who can put forward any sort of objection?

But the parable is not over: there is the elder son, who suddenly explodes in a fit of jealousy.

Let us follow the story that came from the very heart of Christ:

> "Now his older son was in the field, and as he came and drew near to the house, he heard music and dancing. And he called one of the servants and asked what these things meant. And he said to him, 'Your brother has come, and your father has killed the fattened calf, because he has received him back safe and sound.'" (*Luke* 15:25-27).

Elder son! You should run alongside your father! If you really loved him, you should say to him:

> "Father, how happy I am to see you happy! Father, how I share with you the joy of this moment! Father, how merry I feel when I see your heart make merry!"
> And instead: "He was angry and refused to go in." (*Luke* 15:28).

How disappointing this behaviour is! The elder son is not in tune with the father's heart.

He has dug a rift between himself and his father: the

occasion of his brother's return reveals that the rift is as deep as an abyss!

And the father? He has just embraced his younger son once again and already finds himself faced with a new test: he has not yet savoured the merriment of the feast, and he already has to taste the bitterness of a second unexpected departure.

How will he react? How will his indignation explode?

This is what Jesus says: "His father came out and entreated him" (*Luke* 15:28).

No, this is too much! No, this is not dignified!

Yet it is so! This is how God loves, and our life is entirely marked by the expressions of his inexhaustible tenderness: "Son," the father says with his heart in his mouth, "you are always with me, and all that is mine is yours. It was fitting to celebrate and be glad, for this your brother was dead, and is alive; he was lost, and is found" (*Luke* 15:31-32).

Jesus puts the word in the father's mouth: "son"! Jesus, in this way, paints a portrait of God in which Love is the dominant colour that gives life to every other colour: the Father is Love, essentially Love, faithfully Love, inexhaustibly Love.

And we are called to enter into His heart to live His own life:

"O righteous Father," Jesus prays at the supper of great emotions and great confidences, "even though the world does not know you, I know you, and these know that you have sent me. I made known to them your name, and I will continue to make it known, that the love with which you have loved me may be in them, and I in them." (*John* 17:25-26).

Christian prayer sails into this ocean: into the very Love of God! There is no Christian prayer unless our poverty comes into contact with the infinite riches of the Charity of God.

But when prayer is true, a river of love enters our heart and we become full of the Holy Spirit: full of the Love of God! As happened to St Francis of Assisi!

St Francis of Assisi

A Saint moulded of prayer!
This is what accounts for the deep mark
he made on history!
But prayer can also unleash our response
to the Love of God.

St Francis was born in Assisi in 1182. His father, named Pietro di Bernardone, was a very skilful merchant, very wealthy as a result and concerned only with increasing his wealth. His mother, Pica, was of French origin (to be exact, from Provence).

When the child was born, his father was away on business, trading in fabric.

The mother had the child baptised right away and chose the name "Giovanni." When his father returned from his trip, he complained that the name chosen was too religious. And he changed his son's name: he called him "Francesco" in homage to a type of cloth he traded in, which was called "francesco" because it was produced in France.

And so the name "Francesco" entered history. It came in as a name that was chosen in homage to profit! What a strange fact! What a singular fact!

Francis led a carefree, indeed frivolous boyhood. In truth he was never bad-tempered, he was never violent, he was never dirty in his sentiments. In fact, even in his period of frivolity Francis showed himself generous and sensitive towards the poor he met on the street.

It must be said straight off that his father was not happy with this generosity, but he let it go, thinking that sooner or later his spendthrift son would come to his senses on trading and profit, which was the aim of Pietro di Bernardone's life.

Francis's jovial and sociable character won him many friends, and his father's abundant money allowed him to throw all sorts of parties. His peers in Assisi went wild over him and proclaimed him "the party king."

Thus a number of years went by. If he had continued in this way, no one today would talk about him anymore: no one would remember him.

Francis would have been one of the many young people who burn the years away, letting them go up in the flames of selfishness and vanity. If he had kept to this path, St Francis of Assisi would not exist today, and there would be a great void in history.

And instead, no. In the life of the young Francis there is a leap, there is a rupture, there is a change of heart: there is a moment in which Francis becomes different to all of us, and this difference gives him an extraordinary place in history.

St John Paul II, speaking to young people (but the same applies to adults!), one day said, "Don't be like snails!"

At first everyone thought that the pope wanted to urge against keeping a slow pace like snails do. But the pope had a different idea in mind. In fact, he added, "Don't be like snails, which leave behind only a bit of insubstantial and insignificant slime: a little drizzle is enough to wipe out the track of a snail! Don't be like that! Don't squander your life!"

Francis didn't leave behind just a bit of slime; he left a deep furrow. A furrow that is still open and attracts many young people, and raises a question in our hearts: what will we leave behind us? Let's get back to Francis.

Decisive for Francis was the encounter with the Crucified Jesus in the church of San Damiano in the autumn of 1205, when he was 23.

It was an encounter with Jesus who for the first time singled him out, speaking to and entering his heart.

Francis had certainly prayed before the Crucifix many times, but this encounter marked a turning point.

In the lives of many Christians, priests, nuns, theologians, it is precisely this encounter with the living Jesus that is missing, and so Christian life is reduced to a stale habit. God remains distant and almost insignificant: the spark of enthusiasm and the engagement of the heart, and therefore of life, are missing.

But it took a crisis of confidence to set the stage for Francis's decisive encounter with Jesus: Francis soon realised that money is not the sure foundation on which to build life; then he slowly realised that the same was true of amusement, power, success and worldly glory.

Julien Green, struck by the excessive multiplication of places of entertainment that characterises our era, one day had the courage to say, "If one wished to convert, one should go not to church, but to places of 'amusement': there is nothing sadder and more squalid to be found in the world!" And the writer Luigi Santucci exclaimed:

> The pleasure-seekers of this world, the frequenters of nightclubs, sex parties and similar environments, should know that we believers avoid their orgies not so much because we are afraid of hell, but because there is more enjoyment by far in being pure and generous and free from the fetters of selfishness.

Life cannot be built on these foundations because they give way. How many do not understand this!

The worshipper of Psalm 4 exclaims, "O men, how long shall my honour suffer shame? How long will you love vain words, and seek after lies?"

Francis understood all this, and at the same time he discovered his insufficiency, his radical poverty, his fragility, and "stopped worshipping himself" (so relates the *Legend of the Three Companions!*). This attitude would accompany him throughout his life.

"Who are you, my God most sweet? Who am I, most vile worm and your useless servant?", he would repeat continuously in the silence of La Verna.

And in the book of "Little Flowers" we find this enchanting and significant episode:

St Francis once lived in the place of Porziuncola with Brother Masseo da Marignano, a man of great holiness, discretion and grace in speaking about God, for which St Francis loved him very much. One day, when St Francis was coming back from praying in the woods, Brother Masseo wanted to prove how humble he was and went to meet him, and almost mockingly said, "Why you, why you?" St Francis replied, "What is it that you mean?" Brother Masseo said, "'I mean, why does the whole world come after you, and everyone seems to desire to see you and listen to you and obey you? You are not handsome in body, you are not of great learning, you are not noble; why then does the whole world come after you?" At hearing this St Francis was wholly gladdened in spirit and, turning his face up to heaven, remained for a long time with his mind raised to God. Returning to himself, he knelt down and gave praise and thanks to God. And then with great fervour of spirit he turned to Brother Masseo and said, "Do you want to know why the whole world should come after me? This I have from the eyes of the most high God, which everywhere behold the good and the guilty: well, those most holy eyes have not seen among sinners anyone more vile, nor more insufficient, nor a greater sinner than I am." (Fr Francesco Sarri, OFM (ed.), *I fioretti di S. Francesco d'Assisi*, Vallecchi, Florence 1926, pp. 59-60).

The extraordinary fact is that Francis was fully convinced of this. Like St Bernadette, when they asked her why Our Lady had chosen her. Bernadette, with all the sincerity of her heart, replied, "If the Blessed Virgin chose me, it was because I was the most ignorant. If she had found someone more ignorant than I am, it's her she would have chosen" (Fr Charles Sauvé, PSS, *Lourdes intime*, Ancienne Librairie Poussielgue, Paris 1919, p. 249).

In this regard, St Bonaventure relates an episode that reveals Francis's intimate feelings. Here is the enchanting story:

Francis, both in himself and in others, preferred humility to all honours and therefore that God who loves the humble judged him worthy of the most sublime glory, as shown by the vision that came to a very virtuous and devout friar.

One time this travel companion of the man of God, while praying with him in an abandoned church, was caught up in an ecstasy.

He saw many seats in heaven, and among them one more splendid and glorious than all the others, studded with precious stones. Admiring the splendour of that distinguished throne, he began to wonder anxiously who was destined to occupy it. In the midst of these thoughts, he heard a voice telling him, "This seat belonged to one of the rebel angels, and is now reserved for the humble Francis."

Having come back to himself after that ecstatic prayer, the Saint followed the friar, who was leaving the church.

They continued their journey, speaking to each other about God, as was their custom. And then that friar, who had the vision well imprinted in his mind, deftly took the opportunity to ask Francis what opinion he had of himself.

And the humble servant of Christ said to him, "It seems to me that I am the greatest sinner.'" The friar replied that, in all conscience, he could neither think nor say such a thing. But the Saint explained, "If Christ had treated the most wicked of men with the same mercy and goodness with which He has treated me, I am sure that he would be much more grateful to God than I am."

Listening to these humble words, the friar had confirmation that his vision was true, knowing full well that, according to the testimony of the Holy Gospel, the truly humble will be raised to that exalted glory which is withheld from the proud.

Often we perform acts of seeming humility while our hearts remain a den of pride. For Francis, the formidable decision to no longer worship himself readied him for the leap into the arms of God.

Let one thing be quite clear: as long as the self is at the centre, God will always be at the outer edge. Let's not forget it! And when God is at the outer edge, not even brotherhood is possible!

The risk for us is this: pretending to make or to have made the leap towards God, while we keep a foot in both camps, living a life of continuous compromises.

Unfortunately, we all have many hidden "gods," but we don't want to admit it. We must be truthful in ourselves and with ourselves, as Francis was. Only in this way does conversion begin: it begins with an act of true humility, an act of such conviction that it becomes a permanent attitude.

Let's not forget what Francis writes in the *Praise of the Virtues*: "There is absolutely no man in the whole world who can have even one of you [the virtues] if he does not first die [to himself]," that is, if he is not humble.

How can we understand that our security rests entirely on Jesus, and therefore on a solid foundation?

Francis responds in the famous episode of "perfect joy." Let's listen to it carefully:

The same [Brother Leonardo] related that one day Blessed Francis, near Santa Maria [degli Angeli], called Brother Leo and said to him, "Brother Leo, write." He replied, "Here I am, I am ready." "Write," he said, "what true joy is."

"A messenger comes and says that all the professors of Paris have entered the Order; write: this is not true joy. So also, all the prelates from beyond the Alps have entered the Order, not only archbishops and bishops, but even the King of France and the King of England; write: this is not true joy. And if news again reaches you that my friars have gone among the infidels and converted them all to the faith, or that I have received from God enough grace to heal the sick and to perform many miracles; well, I tell you: in all these things there is not true joy."

"But what is true joy?" Brother Leo exclaims.

"Look, I am returning from Perugia and, in the middle of the night, I arrive here and it is a muddy winter so harsh that icicles form at the bottom of my robe and continually strike my legs until they draw blood. And I, all in the mud, in the cold and in the ice, reach the door and, after knocking and calling for a long time, a friar comes and asks, "Who is it?" I reply, "It's Brother Francis." And he says, "Get out of here, this is not a decent time to be going about, you're not coming in." And because I keep insisting, the other replies, "Go away, you're a dolt and an idiot, you can't come in now; there are so many of us that we no longer need you."

And I stand there in front of the door and say, "For the love of God, let me in at least for tonight." And he replies, "I won't. Go to the Brothers of the Cross and try there." Well, if I have had patience and have not got upset, I tell you that here is true joy and here is true virtue and the salvation of the soul."

Let it be quite clear that it is not misunderstandings that bring perfect joy! But if misunderstandings and trials leave me serene, I have the certainty of relying completely on Jesus: and Jesus is faithful and, therefore, my heart will always dwell in "perfect joy." If, however, a misunderstanding or humiliation puts me in distress, it means that my pride is still the sole master of my life: I will never know perfect joy.

Let's return to the San Damiano experience. Francis entered the church of San Damiano with a poor heart, with a heart that had smashed to bits the enemy that we all have inside: pride. And Francis heard Jesus!

St Augustine had the same experience, stating in his *Confessions*: "I was not seeking Jesus as the humble to the humble, and therefore I did not find Him."

In the church of San Damiano, Jesus calls Francis by name: "Francesco!"

And, like a beggar, Jesus tells him: "Francis, repair my house which, as you see, is completely in ruins." Let's look deeper into this extraordinary moment.

In the encounter with Jesus Crucified.

• Francis understood that man has the power to devastate the house of God, because God leaves us truly free: this truth is frightening, but it is essential to understand it. It is possible to become Judas! It is possible! And for everyone! Fr Primo Mazzolari, in a homily one Holy Thursday, courageously said, "Around every Eucharistic Table the shadow of Judas hovers. We must be vigilant and fight so that his shadow and our shadow may not overlap!"

Everyone needs a great deal of humility.

Let's not forget the incisive observation of St Augustine: "God did not create demons, because only good can come from the hands of God. Demons can become such through a free choice. And so it happened. Some of the Angels (created good by God) rebelled against God out of pride: and pride turned some of the Angels into demons." It's a startling fact.

• Francis also understood that God was knocking at the door of his freedom and awaiting his personal response…

as happened to Moses…
as happened to Isaiah…
as happened to Mary…
as happened to the apostles…
as happened to St Paul…
as happened to St Augustine at a friend's country
    house near Milan…
as should happen to us too!

Life is a response. But in order to realise this it is essential to hear the question, the call by name! We are all hard of hearing because there is so much noise of vanity in our hearts! Unfortunately!

• Francis understood that God possesses only the strength of love to persuade us: the Crucifix is a cry of love that spans the centuries, and everyone must perceive it personally. Holiness is unleashed when this cry of love is heard: God has no strength apart from Love, He has no other arguments. This is why, if love is rejected, there is no other way of salvation.

• Francis heard the cry of the Crucified and was wounded by this experience, in which he discovered the power and at the same time the frailty of God-Love.

Tommaso da Celano relates, "From that moment compassion for the Crucified was rooted in his soul… and the venerated stigmata [the wounds of love] were deeply imprinted in his heart."

These are striking words: "He felt compassion for the Crucified." Let us meditate on them, let us meditate on them at length!

And from that moment Francis's life became a response of love to Love! And he would suffer greatly at seeing Love go unloved!

The episode that happened to him near the Porziuncola is significant. Tommaso da Celano further relates:

"Since then he has no longer been able to hold back his tears and even weeps aloud over the Passion of Christ, which is always before his eyes. He fills the streets with sobbing, refusing to be consoled at the memory of Christ's wounds. One day he met a close friend, who on learning of the cause of his pain immediately burst into bitter tears."

The experience of God as "supreme love – supreme good – all good" bestowed on Francis the freedom of poverty as an inevitable consequence: Francis's poverty was not contempt for the things of the world (far from it!), but was a result of the discovery of the true riches, of the true treasure of life, which is God brought near to us in Jesus Crucified for love of us! How important it is to understand this!

His powerful attachment to poverty was for Francis the way of expressing the powerful conviction that God is "the supreme good – all good."

But if God is not perceived as the "supreme good," poverty is impossible…because the heart must be filled somehow. This is terribly true and experience proves it abundantly clear. St Bonaventure relates:

"The Saint, noting how poverty, which had been an intimate friend of the Son of God, was now being repudiated by almost the whole world, wanted to make her his wife, loving her with eternal love, and for her he not only left his father and mother but generously distributed everything he had. No one was as greedy for gold as Francis was greedy for poverty; no one was more eager for treasures than Francis was for this evangelical pearl. Nothing offended his eye more than this: to see something in the friars that was not entirely in harmony with poverty."

These observations of St Bonaventure are striking for their timeliness.

Would that this experience could happen to us too!

Familiarity with the mystery of God brought near to us and made approachable in Jesus revealed to Francis a moving and inalienable characteristic of God: humility! And so the circle is closed: humility is at the beginning and at the end of St Francis's journey.

Yes, God is humble, and from Bethlehem to Calvary everything speaks of the humility of God. And Francis had the courage to address God like this: "You are humility!"

And he cast himself into humility in order to be in communion with God, and felt horror at pride and its wretched daughter, disobedience. St Bonaventure relates:

"He once said to a companion, 'It will not seem to me that I am a friar minor if I am not in the state that I am now about to describe to you.

'Look: I am the superior of the friars and I go to the chapter; I preach and admonish the friars and in the end they start saying against me, You are not fit for us; you are not educated, you don't know how to speak, you are a dolt and an idiot! In the end I am ignominiously chased away, amid the insults of all. I tell you: if I do not listen to all this with the same expression, with the same delight of spirit and with the same purpose of holiness, I am not a friar minor at all.'"

And he added, "'In the prelature, downfall; in praise, the precipice; in the humble state of subject, gain for the soul. How in the world, then, are we more inclined to danger than to gain, since this lifetime has been granted to us that we may gain?'" Precisely for this reason, Francis, a model of humility, wanted his friars to be called Minor and the prelates of his Order to have the name of Ministers. In this way he made use of words contained in the Gospel, which he had promised to observe, while his disciples, from their name, learned that they had come to the school of the humble Christ, to learn humility. And humility also became the style of his apostolate.
It is related in the *Legend of Perugia*:

Some friars once said to Francis, "Father, don't you see that the Bishops sometimes do not allow us to preach, forcing us to remain idle for days in certain cities, before we can speak to the people? It would be more convenient if you would get us a charter from the Lord Pope, for the benefit of the salvation of souls. Francis replied in an annoyed tone, "You, friars minor, do not know the will of God and are not allowing me to convert the whole world in the way desired by God. In fact, I intend first of all to convert the prelates with humility and respect. And when they remark our holy life and the reverence with which we surround them, they themselves will implore you to preach and convert the people. And they will draw to you people better than the charters you covet, which would lead you to become proud. If you are free from any self-interest and persuade the people to respect the rights of the churches, the prelates will ask you to hear the confessions of their faithful. Besides, you needn't worry about this: those who convert have no trouble finding confessors. For myself I want this charter from the Lord: not to have any charter from men, apart from that of being respectful towards all and of converting people more with example than with words, in conformity with the ideal of the Rule."

And, precisely because he was humble, Francis did not become violent, a revolutionary, a protester: he became a reformer with the power of example, with the power of holiness.

G K Chesterton said one day, "If the level of humility among men increased, even a little, you cannot imagine how good life in this world would be." This also applies to us Christians and to all men.

At this point we can ask ourselves: but what is the message that Francis leaves to all Christians and all men?

It is simple, and at the same time formidable: Francis invites us to take the Gospel seriously, to take Jesus seriously, to take seriously the path Jesus followed, because love makes alike: love generates imitation!

St Francis reminds us that the Gospel is liveable! The question comes: do we really love the Lord? Is the Lord truly our good and our supreme good? Let's not respond hastily.

The problem lies entirely here. May God's Mercy grant us to make the leap towards God, towards the Love of God, just as Francis did. It's our turn now. Francis himself reminds us of this with the words he addressed to the friars shortly before leaving this earth:

> When he felt the last days were near, in which the ephemeral light would be succeeded by the eternal light, he showed by the example of his virtues that he had nothing in common with the world. Exhausted by that illness so grave that it put an end to all his suffering, he had himself laid naked on the bare ground, to be prepared in that final hour, in which the enemy could still unleash his rage, to fight naked with a naked adversary. In reality he fearlessly awaited the triumph, and in his joined hands he clasped the crown of justice. Placed thus on the ground and stripped of his sackcloth, he raised, as always, his face to heaven, and, with his gaze fixed entirely on that glory, he covered the wound on his right side with his left hand, so that it could not be seen. Then he said to the friars, "I have done my duty; as for yours, may Christ instruct you in it!"

Today Francis addresses these words to each of us.

Now it is our turn to give a response of love to the infinite love that stands before us, driven into the ground of our life with the Cross of Jesus crucified for our love.

The Church of San Damiano is within each of us: there Jesus calls us by name and awaits our response. And we can only hear the voice of Jesus by praying: praying truly, praying humbly.

Brothers and sisters, I invite you all to return to the school of prayer. See to it that your prayer becomes more true, more nourished by the Gospel, more open to listening and less swamped by questions.

Dear parents, I ask you for a small commitment: bring prayer back into your families, starting with a moment of communion between the two of you every evening, at the end of your day.

And, slowly, bring prayer back to the beginning of every meal you share with your children: you will look on each other with new eyes and you will realise that prayer gives a different flavour to life. Try it!

Pray, and you will have a different gaze and a different heart. I tell you this with intimate conviction and with the desire to see reflected in your eyes the Light of God that you have welcomed into your hearts.

Mother Teresa of Calcutta

She said at the UN, "I am just a poor nun who prays!"
This is the definition that the Mother gave of herself.
Malcolm Muggeridge

Malcolm Muggeridge, a rather smug and indifferent English journalist, went to Calcutta in 1969 with the simple and innocuous aim of shooting a film on the life of Mother Teresa and her nuns, inside the "House of the Immaculate Heart," which some Europeans called, with a bit of disdain, "Calcutta's House of the Deathbound."

Malcolm, who did not have faith, asked permission to film life as it took place inside the two big rooms where many poor people, many sick people, many dying people were brought daily. Right away something inexplicable happened. Here is his account:

> Part of the work of the Sisters is to pick up the dying from the streets of Calcutta, and bring them into a building given to Mother Teresa for the purpose (a sometime temple dedicated to the cult of the goddess Kali), there, as she puts it, to die within sight of a loving

face. Some do die; others survive and are cared for. This Home for the Dying is dimly lit by small windows high up in the walls, and Ken [Macmillan, the cameraman] was adamant that filming was quite impossible there. We had only one small light with us, and to get the place adequately lighted in the time at our disposal was quite impossible. It was decided that, nonetheless, Ken should have a go, but by way of insurance he took as well some film in an outside courtyard where some of the inmates were sitting in the sun. In the processed film, the part taken inside was bathed in a particularly beautiful soft light, whereas the part taken outside was rather dim and confused.

How to account for this? Ken has all along insisted that, technically speaking, the result is impossible. To prove the point, on his next filming expedition – to the Middle East – he used some of the same stock in a similarly poor light, with completely negative results. He offers no explanation, but just shrugs and agrees that it happened. I myself am absolutely convinced that the technically unaccountable light is, in fact, the Kindly Light Newman refers to in his well-known exquisite hymn. (Malcolm Muggeridge, *Something Beautiful for God*, Harper & Row, New York 1986, pp. 41, 44).

But the real miracle was another. Malcolm Muggeridge carefully observed what was happening in the two large dormitories, and then ventured to say to Mother Teresa, "Mother, there is enough here to have hell on earth. Here there is poverty, here there are malnourished people, here there are skeletons covered only by skin, here there is death, you can look it in the face. Yet here, everyone smiles, here there is no desperation, but joy of living. Mother, why?"

Mother Teresa was feeding a poor, malnourished woman who had just been picked up from the street. She stopped for a few moments, looked at the journalist, and then replied, "Here there is no hell, here there is heaven because here there is love!" Then, with serenity, she continued to feed the woman, who had her mouth open like that of a child waiting for their mother's milk.

Malcolm Muggeridge was struck. And, since he was intellectually honest, he wanted to delve into the mystery of that unusual holiness, and asked, "But where do you find the strength to love, where do you find the strength to smile…here?" Mother Teresa was extremely sincere, and she challenged the journalist, saying to him, "Come tomorrow, at six in the morning, to the door of our little convent. You will understand where we find the strength to love and to smile." The next day, punctually like a true Englishman, Malcolm was at the door of the little convent.

Mother Teresa, also punctual, welcomed him and led him into the barebones chapel, without pews to sit on, where a group of nuns wearing the saris of women who count for nothing in India were gathered in prayer and awaited the celebration of Holy Mass.

Malcolm Muggeridge participated in silence, and to him everything seemed simple, humble, and also a bit mysterious and a bit boring.

He wondered: "What are these nuns doing? Whom are they talking to? What do they receive in that little host? Could it be possible that the whole secret is here?" After Holy Mass, while Mother Teresa was walking quickly to her poor, she said to the journalist, "Did you see? The whole secret is here. It is Jesus who puts His Love in our hearts, and we simply go and give it to the poor we meet on our way."

Do you know what the conclusion was? After a while the indifferent journalist asked to receive Holy Baptism and to become Catholic, with this wonderful motivation: "I want to become Catholic to receive the Holy Eucharist that produces, in that holy woman, such a miracle of love and joy."

And that is what happened. Love lived out brought Malcolm Muggeridge into the arms of Living Love, which is Jesus.

Why don't our Communions produce this effect? Let's think seriously about that.

Let us stay on the trail of this "nun who prays."

When in 1979 the news came out that the Nobel Peace Prize had been awarded to Mother Teresa of Calcutta, it came as a great surprise. It was not surprising that the prize was awarded to Mother Teresa. On the contrary. Who deserved it more than she did?

But the surprise arose from the fact that a strictly Lutheran committee had decided to award the Nobel Peace Prize to a Catholic nun: truly the Holy Spirit blows where He wills!

It must be said right away that Mother Teresa had no love for prizes. She accepted them to make the poor known and to be able to help the poor: no other reason would have persuaded her.

When she was about to leave for Oslo, where she would be given the Nobel Peace Prize in December 1979, a few people were bent on giving Mother advice which, humanly speaking, was more than reasonable. They said to her, "Mother, the Nobel Peace Prize was born on Lutheran soil. And the award ceremony takes place in the Oslo parliament, which is a Lutheran parliament. So it is not appropriate for you to show up with rosary beads in your hand: the Lutherans, in fact, reject devotion to Our Lady as superstition. Unfortunately, that's the way it is!"

Mother Teresa listened in silence. When the day of the award ceremony came, the Mother showed up clutching in her scrawny hands the biggest rosary she had: this was not a provocation, it was her identity; it was not ostentation, but straightforward consistency.

The Mother accepted the award in all simplicity and gave a memorable speech from her heart, which made some people grimace, but revealed, once again, the profound convictions that guided all her actions. Did they want to reward her actions? Well! Then they had to know where her actions came from. Mother Teresa's profound honesty truly shines here.

And the last words Mother Teresa spoke at the Nobel Peace Prize award ceremony are a heartfelt appeal to pray that eyes may be opened to the terrible and pervasive crime of abortion.

She said this: "And so today, I ask His Majesties here before you all who come from different countries, let us all pray that we have the courage to stand by the unborn child, and give the child an opportunity to love and to be loved, and I think with God's grace we will be able to bring peace in the world."

But Providence willed that Mother Teresa should speak at the UN Assembly itself.

The objectives of the UN are largely, if not exclusively, political. As is well known, Mother Teresa always tried to steer clear of party politics.

It does not appear that she ever took the initiative in direct or indirect relations with the UN. It appears instead from the documents that the UN, through its secretary general Javier Pérez de Cuéllar, took the initiative to invite her to a public event that took place on 26 October 1985. On that occasion, in addition to commemorating the fortieth anniversary of the foundation of the international body, the UN wanted to pay homage to her by screening a documentary entitled *The World of Mother Teresa*, directed by Canadian filmmaker Ann Petrie.

Pérez de Cuéllar introduced Mother Teresa to all those attending the ceremony, to which the then archbishop of New York, Cardinal John O'Connor, had been invited. Perhaps among all the definitions given, in life and after death, of Mother Teresa – all more or less related to the holiness of her life, to her generosity in service to the poorest of the poor – that of Pérez de Cuéllar was the most surprising and paradoxical. Pérez de Cuéllar said that Mother Teresa was "the most powerful woman in the world." Here are his words:

> "This is a hall of words. A few days ago we had, in this rostrum, the most powerful men in the world. Now we have the privilege to have the most powerful woman in the world. I don't think I need to present her. She doesn't need words. She does need deeds. I think that the best thing I can do is to pay tribute to her and to tell [say] that she is much more than I, much more than all of us. She is the United Nations. She is peace in this world". (Leo M. Maasburg, *Mother Teresa of Calcutta*, Ignatius Press, San Francisco 2011, p. 176).

Mother Teresa, faced with these grandiose words, shrank even smaller, but her faith was great and her courage was equally great.

She displayed the inevitable rosary and said, "I am just a poor nun who prays. In prayer, Jesus puts His love in my heart and I go to give it to all the poor I meet on my way."

There was a moment of silence, which seemed like an eternity. Then she added, "You pray too! Pray, and you will notice the poor around you. Perhaps on your own doorstep. Perhaps even in your homes there is someone waiting for your love. Pray and your eyes will open and your heart will be filled with love."

Tell me if this woman didn't have the courage of a lion! And where did she find the courage? In prayer!

Let us follow her example: may this year dedicated to prayer awaken in each of us the humility that brings us to our knees and makes a true prayer come from our hearts.

When Michelangelo was asked how he sculpted the famous David, he replied, "It was simple! All it took was to remove the marble that hid the masterpiece!"

The same thing can happen to you too – praying! Let go of a little pride, pray with great faith and humility, and the masterpiece that God has carved inside you will come out.